WOULD YOU RATHER?

WOULD YOU RATHER...?

Swim in a Jello lake?

- OR -

Climb an ice cream mountain?

- OR -

Play on a sugar beach?

WOULD YOU RATHER...?

Have spaghetti for hair?

- OR -

Have corn for teeth?

- OR -

Have potato chips for fingernails?

WOULD YOU RATHER...?

Climb a tree covered in spiders?

- OR -

Go swimming sharks?

- OR -

Ride a bike next to a big cliff?

WOULD YOU RATHER...?

Have the wings of a bat?

- OR -

Have the teeth of a bat?

- OR -

Have the eyes of a bat?

WOULD YOU RATHER...?

Get lost at the beach?

- OR -

Get lost at an amusement park?

- OR -

Get lost in the woods?

WOULD YOU RATHER...?

Have an elephant for a pet?

 -OR-

Have a giraffe for a pet?

 -OR-

Have an alligator for a pet?

WOULD YOU RATHER...?

Be an angry monkey?

Be a sad puppy?

Be an afraid tiger?

WOULD YOU RATHER...?

Slide down a waterfall?

- OR -

Swing over a cliff?

- OR -

Climb the monkey bars over a river?

WOULD YOU RATHER...?

Change your first name?

- OR -

Change your middle name?

- OR -

Change your last name?

WOULD YOU RATHER...?

Drive a bus?

- OR -

Operate a train?

- OR -

Fly a plane?

WOULD YOU RATHER...?

Write a book?

-OR-

Play in a band?

-OR-

Act in a play?

WOULD YOU RATHER...?

Take amazing photos?

- OR -

Draw awesome picture?

- OR -

Write incredible poems?

WOULD YOU RATHER...?

Dance with your legs?

-OR-

Dance with your hips?

-OR-

Dance with your hands?

WOULD YOU RATHER...?

Have the softest pillow in the world?

=OR=

Have the softest blanket in the world?

=OR=

Have the softest mattress in the world?

WOULD YOU RATHER...?

Lose your voice?

-OR-

Lose the ability to read?

-OR-

Lose the ability to write?

WOULD YOU RATHER...?

Be fluent in Spanish?

- OR -

Be fluent in French?

- OR -

Be fluent in English?

WOULD YOU RATHER...?

Have mice?

-OR-

Have bedbugs?

-OR-

Have termites?

WOULD YOU RATHER...?

Live at the top of a tower?

- OR -

Live on a boat?

- OR -

Live in a cave?

WOULD YOU RATHER...?

Have a triceratops as a pet?

-OR-

Have a brontosaurus as a pet?

-OR-

Have a T-Rex as a pet?

WOULD YOU RATHER...?

Eat tacos?

-OR-

Eat burritos?

-OR-

Eat quesadillas?

WOULD YOU RATHER...?

Find a leprechaun?

- OR -

Find a genie's lamp?

- OR -

Have a fairy godmother?

WOULD YOU RATHER...?

Have scissors for hands?

- OR -

Have crayons for fingers?

- OR -

Have paperclips for fingernails?

WOULD YOU RATHER...?

Not be able to eat cold food?

- OR -

Not be able to eat hot food?

- OR -

Not be able to eat sweet food?

WOULD YOU RATHER...?

Receive the silent treatment?

Get yelled at?

Get publicly scolded?

WOULD YOU RATHER...?

loat like a cloud?

- OR -

Flow like the wind?

- OR -

Flutter like a snowflake?

WOULD YOU RATHER...?

Have a self-driving car?

Have a self-cooking stove?

Have a self-cleaning house?

WOULD YOU RATHER...?

Eat dirt?

-OR-

Eat sand?

-OR-

Eat a bug?

WOULD YOU RATHER...?

Catch fireflies?

- OR -

Catch butterflies?

- OR -

Catch worms?

WOULD YOU RATHER...?

Have a perfectly-tended garden?

- OR -

Have a perfectly-mowed lawn?

- OR -

Have a perfectly-painted house?

WOULD YOU RATHER...?

Have a pet dog?

OR

Have a pet cat?

OR

Have a pet fish?

WOULD YOU RATHER...?

Have skylights?

-OR-

Have a fireplace?

-OR-

Have a pool table?

WOULD YOU RATHER...?

Have tea with the Queen of England?

Have dinner with the President of the United States?

Eat breakfast with the Pope?

WOULD YOU RATHER...?

Ride a bike with
a flat tire?

- OR -

Ride a bike without handle
bars?

- OR -

Ride a bike with
out pedals?

WOULD YOU RATHER...?

Have feet that never stop growing?

Have a nose that never stops growing?

Have ears that never stop growing?

WOULD YOU RATHER...?

Eat wild mushrooms?

- OR -

Eat wild berries?

- OR -

Eat wild seeds?

WOULD YOU RATHER...?

Go on a walk with Bigfoot?

 - OR -

Go fishing with the Loch Ness Monster?

- OR -

Go sledding with the Abominable Snowman?

WOULD YOU RATHER...?

Eat authentic Mexican tacos?

-OR-

Eat authentic Japanese sushi?

-OR-

Eat authentic Italian pasta?

WOULD YOU RATHER...?

Be able to see what others see?

- OR -

Be able to hear what others hear?

- OR -

Be able to feel what others feel?

WOULD YOU RATHER...?

Live in a house made of ice?

- OR -

Live in a house made of straw?

- OR -

Live in a house made of mud?

WOULD YOU RATHER...?

Be a master guitar player?

-OR-

Be a piano-playing prodigy?

-OR-

Be incredible on the drums?

WOULD YOU RATHER...?

Wear mismatched socks?

 **-OR-**

Wear a shirt with a missing button?

 **-OR-**

Wear pants with a hole in them?

WOULD YOU RATHER...?

Have unlimited funds for food?

- OR -

Have unlimited funds for clothes?

- OR -

Have unlimited funds for travel?

WOULD YOU RATHER...?

Create world peace?

- OR -

End world hunger?

- OR -

End world poverty?

WOULD YOU RATHER...?

Only need to sleep three hours a day?

Only need to eat one meal a day?

Never be too hot or too cold?

WOULD YOU RATHER...?

Pierce your ears?

-OR-

Dye your hair?

-OR-

Get a tattoo?

WOULD YOU RATHER...?

Be a teacher?

- OR -

Be a nurse?

- OR -

Be a banker

WOULD YOU RATHER...?

Be able to take away people's sadness?

 - OR -

Be able to take away people's pain?

 - OR -

Be able to take away people's sickness?

WOULD YOU RATHER...?

Be in a hotdog-eating contest?

- OR -

Be in a pie-eating contest?

- OR -

Be in a chicken wing-eating contest?

WOULD YOU RATHER....?

Have a lightbulb that never burns out?

- OR -

Have a battery that never dies?

- OR -

Have a pen that never runs out of ink?

WOULD YOU RATHER...?

Go to school on Saturday?

= OR =

Stay in school one hour later every day?

= OR =

Sit with your teacher every lunch break?

WOULD YOU RATHER...?

Eat cantaloupe?

- OR -

Eat watermelon?

 - OR -

Eat honeydew?

WOULD YOU RATHER...?

Have a million Twitter followers?

-OR-

Have a million Instagram followers?

-OR-

Have a million Facebook friends?

WOULD YOU RATHER...?

Have a waterproof mobile phone?

- OR -

Have a mobile phone that can fall any distance without breaking?

- OR -

Have a mobile phone that you could never lose?

WOULD YOU RATHER...?

Never eat food with gluten?

Never eat meat?

Never eat dairy

WOULD YOU RATHER...?

Be really good at math?

 - OR -

Be really good at reading

- OR -

Be really good at science?

WOULD YOU RATHER...?

Eat strawberries?

- OR -

Eat blueberries?

- OR -

Eat raspberries?

WOULD YOU RATHER...?

Be able to unlock any door?

- OR -

Be able to hack any password?

- OR -

Be able to drive any vehicle?

WOULD YOU RATHER...?

Know the definition of every word?

Know how to cook any meal?

Know how to build any invention?

WOULD YOU RATHER...?

Not be able to see your reflection?

= OR =

Not be able to see other people's reflections?

= OR =

Only be able to see your reflection, and nothing else, when you looked in a mirror?

WOULD YOU RATHER...?

Be able to recharge any battery with your mind?

 **-OR-**

Be able to power any device with a smile?

 **-OR-**

Be able to fix anything with a clap?

WOULD YOU RATHER...?

Eat dog food?

- OR -

Eat cat food?

 - OR -

Eat fish food?

WOULD YOU RATHER...?

Have an eraser that could erase ink?

-OR-

Have tape that could stick to anything?

-OR-

Have a crayon that could draw in any color?

WOULD YOU RATHER...?

Always walk up the stairs on your hands and knees?

- OR -

Always open a door with your eyes closed?

- OR -

Always enter a room backwards?

WOULD YOU RATHER...?

Swim with sharks?

- OR -

Dance with wolves?

- OR -

Crawl with snakes?

WOULD YOU RATHER...?

Have a picnic in Central Park?

- OR -

Enjoy a drink on the Eiffel Tower?

- OR -

Eat ice cream at the Taj Mahal?

WOULD YOU RATHER...?

Share an Uber with a clown?

- OR -

Take a bus with a mime?

- OR -

Ride in a taxi with a magician?

WOULD YOU RATHER...?

Have a trampoline in your backyard?

-OR-

Have a pool in your backyard?

-OR-

Have a treehouse in your backyard?

WOULD YOU RATHER...?

Have hardwood floors?

- OR -

Have exposed brick?

- OR -

Have marble countertop?

WOULD YOU RATHER...?

Be able to store your dreams in a bottle?

- OR -

Be able to lock your memories in a box?

- OR -

Be able to keep your thoughts in a jar?

WOULD YOU RATHER...?

Be able to make things disappear?

=OR=

Be able to read minds?

=OR=

Be able to unlock any lock?

WOULD YOU RATHER...?

Eat strawberry ice cream?

- OR -

Eat vanilla ice cream?

- OR -

Eat chocolate ice cream?

WOULD YOU RATHER...?

Have the best jokes in your family?

= OR =

Have the smelliest farts in your family?

= OR =

Have the best stories in your family?

WOULD YOU RATHER...?

Be able to navigate anywhere without using a map?

- OR -

Be able to find anyone?

- OR -

Be able to travel for free?

Get married?

-OR-

Have kids?

-OR-

Buy a house?

Made in the
USA
Middletown, DE